HOW DID IT HA~~PPEN?~~

THE FIRST WORLD WAR

R. G. Grant

W
FRANKLIN WAT~~TS~~
LONDON • SYDNEY

First published in 2005 by Franklin Watts
Reprinted 2007

Copyright © 2005 Arcturus Publishing Limited

Franklin Watts
338 Euston Road, London NW1 3BH

Franklin Watts Australia
Level 17/207 Kent Street, Sydney, NSW 2000

Produced by Arcturus Publishing Ltd
26/27 Bickels Yard, 151–153 Bermondsey Street
London SE1 3HA

Series concept: Alex Woolf
Editor: Rebecca Gerlings
Designer: Stonecastle Graphics
Picture researcher: Thomas Mitchell

Picture credits:
All images copyright of Getty Images

A CIP catalogue record for this book is available
from the British Library

Dewey Decimal Classification Number: 940.3

ISBN: 978-0-7496-7290-4

Printed in China

Franklin Watts is a division of Hachette
Children's Books

Contents

1 The Origins of the War

In 1914, the major powers of Europe – Britain, Germany, France, Austria-Hungary and Russia – had been at peace for more than 40 years. But it was an armed peace. All the major powers sought to achieve security by having bigger armies and better armaments than their rivals. On the European mainland, countries imposed compulsory military service on their male population, and were prepared to mobilize armies of millions of men in days. Peace was maintained only by the threat of war.

The last war between two of the major powers had occurred in 1870–71, when the Germans, led by the king of Prussia, defeated France, annexing the French provinces of Alsace and Lorraine. As a result of this victory, the powerful German Empire was created, with the Prussian king as its emperor or 'Kaiser'. The defeat of 1871 left France with a fear of German military might, and a strong desire to recover Alsace-Lorraine. In 1894, the French Republic formed an alliance with the Russian Empire, which also feared German power and had conflicts with Germany's ally, the Habsburg-ruled Austro-Hungarian Empire. The tension between the Franco-Russian alliance and the Central Powers – Germany and Austria-Hungary – became a fixed feature of European international relations.

Britain stood aside from European alliances, relying on its powerful navy to make it secure from invasion. But, during the early

Launched in 1906, the British battleship HMS *Dreadnought* had the most powerful guns of any warship in the world. The building of *Dreadnought*, and other battleships of its class, was part of a naval arms race between Britain and Germany.

VOICES FROM THE PAST

Dangerous arms race

In 1899, Tsar Nicholas II, the ruler of Russia, warned that the arms race in Europe – the constant struggle to produce larger armies, heavier guns and bigger warships – would one day lead to war instead of preserving peace:

'The accelerating arms race is transforming the armed peace into a crushing burden that weighs on all nations, and if prolonged, will lead to the very cataclysm it seeks to avert.'

John Keegan, *The First World War* (Hutchinson, 1998)

years of the twentieth century, the British became increasingly worried about the rising power of Germany. In 1900, the Germans embarked on a programme of warship building which challenged British supremacy at sea. The British responded by engaging in a naval arms race with Germany. Also, in 1904, Britain negotiated an *entente cordiale* with France – an informal agreement on issues that might cause tension between the two countries. Britain did not sign an alliance but, over the following decade, British and French military leaders did form plans to resist a possible German attack.

Both Britain and France ruled large colonial empires in Africa and Asia. Germany, however, despite the power of its economy and military forces, had only a small overseas empire. This was a source of discontent for the Germans. Germany's efforts to expand its influence outside Europe threatened British and French interests. For example, in 1905, and again in 1911, Germany tried to contest French influence in Morocco. These confrontations were ultimately settled by compromise but, in 1911 in particular, brought Europe to the very brink of war.

France reacted to what it saw as threats from Germany by introducing radical plans in 1913 to expand the size of its conscript

Before the war, the major confrontation in Europe was between the Central Powers, or German and Austro-Hungarian Empires, and France and the Russian Empire. After war broke out, the UK joined the side of France and Russia, and Belgium and Serbia were invaded by the Central Powers.

army. Russia was also growing in military strength. To German leaders, who complained of 'encirclement' by Russia and France, it seemed that their potential enemies were growing dangerously stronger.

The fatal crisis eventually came in the Balkans. Here, two wars involving Balkan states and the Ottoman Empire were fought in 1912–13. They resulted in a great increase in the power and territory of Serbia. As Slavs, the Serbs were supported by Russia, the leading Slav power. But their increasing strength was deeply worrying to Austria-Hungary, which had a large Slav minority among its multinational population, and which had annexed Bosnia and Herzegovina – provinces with a substantial Serb population – in 1908.

Rush to War

When the Austrian Archduke Franz Ferdinand – heir to the Austro-Hungarian throne – was shot by a Serb nationalist during a visit to Bosnia on 28 June 1914, key Austro-Hungarian military and political leaders were eager to make the assassination the pretext for declaring war on Serbia. They believed that a military victory over the upstart Slav state would strengthen the Habsburg empire. The Austrian emperor, Franz Josef, was more cautious. He insisted on consulting his German allies. The German emperor, Kaiser Wilhelm II, assured Austria-Hungary that it could 'rely on Germany's full support'.

The bodies of Archduke Franz Ferdinand, heir to the throne of Austria-Hungary, and his wife, are displayed after their assassination in Sarajevo. The killings, carried out by a Bosnian Serb, gave the Austro-Hungarian government an excuse for declaring war on Serbia.

Europe's leaders were slow to appreciate the seriousness of the situation. The Kaiser left for his summer yachting holiday as planned. It was almost a month after the assassination before the Austro-Hungarian government made its move. On 23 July, it sent an ultimatum to the Serbian government, threatening to declare war unless a series of humiliating demands were met. The Serbs agreed to

TURNING POINT

Assassination in Sarajevo

On 28 June 1914, Archduke Franz Ferdinand, heir to the throne of Austria-Hungary, visited Sarajevo, in the province of Bosnia. Among the crowds gathered to see the archduke were six young Bosnians who intended to kill him. They wanted to free Bosnia from Austro-Hungarian rule and make it part of Serbia instead. Their first attempt to kill the archduke with a bomb failed. But later in the day, by chance, the archduke's car stopped near a shop where one of the young Bosnians, 19-year-old Gavrilo Princip, had gone to buy a sandwich. He pulled out a gun and shot the archduke and his wife. Their deaths were the spark that ignited the First World War.

most of the demands but not all. Austria-Hungary declared war on Serbia on 28 July. Russia meanwhile put its army on a war footing in readiness to support the Serbs.

The Austro-Hungarian declaration of war on Serbia led with breathtaking speed to a general European war. All countries' war plans were based on moving massive numbers of troops to the border by train and throwing them into the attack as quickly as possible. Their fear was that the enemy would get an attack in first, before they had time to complete the complicated process of mobilization. Germany felt itself in an especially difficult situation, because it expected to have to fight a war on two fronts – against Russia in the east and France in the west. Germany's war plan, the Schlieffen Plan, was based on achieving a rapid victory over France before the massive but inefficient Russian army could get into action. This seemed to the German generals their only hope of success.

Once the Russians began to mobilize their troops, the German generals felt they must put the Schlieffen Plan into immediate effect, even though Russia's intention was only to oppose an Austro-Hungarian attack on Serbia. The Kaiser contacted his cousin, Tsar Nicholas II of Russia, on 29 July with an appeal for peace, to which the Tsar responded positively. But General Helmuth von Moltke, head of the German general staff, in effect overruled his emperor, arguing that to interrupt war preparations would leave Germany exposed to a Russian invasion.

Future enemies, Tsar Nicholas II of Russia (left) and Germany's Kaiser Wilhelm II (right) ride side by side in a royal carriage about two years before the war. All the royal heads of state in Europe were closely related – for example, Kaiser Wilhelm was cousin to both Tsar Nicholas and Britain's King George V.

VOICES FROM THE PAST

Conflicting emotions

A British soldier described the mixed emotions of crowds watching him and his colleagues leave for the war at the port of Felixstowe in August 1914:

'[People were] cheering, shouting, singing, waving their handkerchiefs ... Some of the young girls were even pelting us with flowers ... I turned up my head and found myself inches from a woman who was staring into my face ... As I went by I could see that she had tears in her eyes.'

Lyn Macdonald, *1914: The Days of Hope* (Penguin, 1989)

Civilians who have volunteered to join the British Army shortly after the outbreak of the war are escorted through the streets by soldiers in uniform. In the autumn of 1914, the British Army received about 30,000 new recruits every day.

On 1 August, Germany declared war on Russia after the Russians refused to halt mobilization. Two days later, Germany declared war on France, having failed to obtain a promise from the French to keep out of the war. Whether Britain would enter the conflict was at that point still uncertain. Some British leaders felt that

HOW DID IT HAPPEN?

Was Germany responsible for starting the war?

Some historians have argued that Germany started the First World War in order to achieve military domination of Europe. Immanuel Geiss wrote: 'Germany was the aggressor ... deliberately provoking Russia. This drove Russia, France and Britain ... into a position where they could not but react against massive German ambitions.' Others have agreed that Germany played the leading part in starting the war, but because of fears for its own security. The German leaders, it is argued, feared the growing power of Russia, and decided it was best to fight in 1914, while they still had a chance of victory, rather than later, when they would lose.

Many historians, however, hold that Europe slipped into war more or less by accident, and that Germany deserves no special blame. Military historian Richard Holmes, for example, wrote that Europe's 'political and military leaders were wrestling with problems quite beyond their resources' and that the events leading up to the war were a 'calamity' that no one could control.

Niall Ferguson, *The Pity of War (Penguin, 1998)*; Richard Holmes, *The Western Front* (BBC, 1999)

Britain must go to war in support of France to maintain a 'balance of power' in Europe. They believed that if Germany dominated the European mainland, this would be a threat to British independence. But others believed Britain should stay out of a continental war. The issue was settled, however, when Germany invaded neutral Belgium on 4 August – a necessary part of implementing the Schlieffen Plan. Britain had guaranteed Belgium's neutrality and declared war on Germany in its defence.

In going to war, governments enjoyed the overwhelming support of their people. Cheering, flag-waving crowds filled the centres of major cities across Europe and where they were not forced into armies by conscription, thousands of men rushed to volunteer to fight. Of course, many people also felt dismayed and fearful at the prospect of a general war. But in all combatant countries, on both sides of the conflict, the vast majority of people believed that the war was being fought for a just cause and in self-defence.

2 Not Over by Christmas

In August 1914, some 6 million men were mobilized for war on the European continent. Field Marshall Lord Horatio Herbert Kitchener, made British Secretary of State for War at the start of the conflict, told the British government that the war would probably last from 3 to 4 years. But this was not what most people expected. The general belief was that the war would be decided quickly by a series of immensely destructive but rapidly fought battles. It would be 'all over by Christmas'.

At first, it seemed there might indeed be a quick end to the conflict. Within less than a month of the war's starting, Germany appeared to have victory within its grasp. Implementing the Schlieffen Plan, the Germans concentrated the major part of their forces on an offensive through Belgium. The small Belgian army resisted gallantly, slowing the Germans' progress, but the invaders soon broke through and advanced towards the French border. On the way, German soldiers burned down some villages and towns, and executed groups of civilians suspected of acts of resistance. These atrocities in Belgium turned many people who were neutral, especially in the United States, against Germany.

German soldiers march through the Belgian capital, Brussels, in August 1914. Germany's invasion of neutral Belgium and its sometimes brutal behaviour towards the Belgian people shocked world opinion.

Meanwhile, in mid-August, the French army began an offensive in Lorraine, intending to break through the German defences and surge into Germany. The offensive was a catastrophe. The French infantry and cavalry, in their bright blue uniforms, launched themselves in mass attacks upon German fortified positions. They were massacred by machine-guns, rapid rifle fire and artillery. The French lost hundreds of thousands of troops in this Battle of the Frontiers, and were driven back in disarray.

By 20 August, British troops shipped across the English Channel had taken up a position on the extreme left of the French line. The British Expeditionary Force (BEF) was small by continental standards – a little over 100,000 men – because Britain did not have compulsory military service, depending instead on a small professional army. The BEF found itself directly in the path of the far more powerful German forces advancing through Belgium. On 24 August, the British troops encountered the advancing Germans at Mons. After putting up valiant resistance, the BEF was forced to withdraw. With their French allies, the British retreated through the rest of August, falling back towards Paris.

While the Germans looked triumphant on the Western Front, they seemed in trouble in the east. The basis of German strategy was the hope that victory in the west could be achieved before the Russian

Members of the British Expeditionary Force, along with Belgian soldiers, retreat after the Battle of Mons. Although fighting valiantly, the BEF and the Belgians were unable to hold their positions in the face of the overwhelming power of the German onslaught.

VOICES FROM THE PAST

The shock of war

Charles de Gaulle, a future president of France, was a captain in the French army in 1914. He described the shock felt by French troops – brought up to believe that bravery was the key to victory in war – when they first encountered German firepower:

'Suddenly the enemy's fire became precise and concentrated. Second by second the hail of bullets and the thunder of shells grew stronger. Those who survived lay flat on the ground, amid the screaming wounded and the humble corpses ... In an instant it had become clear that not all the courage in the world could withstand this fire.'

Richard Holmes, *The Western Front* (BBC, 1999)

forces could mount a serious attack on Germany. But the Russians mobilized far faster and more effectively than the Germans had thought possible. By 17 August, Russian armies were advancing into German territory in East Prussia. The Germans responded to this crisis by appointing Field Marshal Paul von Hindenburg to command the Eastern Front, with General Erich Ludendorff as his chief of staff. They also transferred some troops from the Western Front to strengthen their forces in the east.

German Field Marshal Paul von Hindenburg (centre), and his chief of staff, General Erich Ludendorff (right), became national heroes in Germany after their victory over the Russians at Tannenberg on 26–31 August 1914.

Victory in the East

The Germans were heavily outnumbered by the Russians in East Prussia but, by skilful manoeuvring, Hindenburg and Ludendorff achieved a devastating victory at the battle of Tannenberg on 26–31 August. Around 100,000 Russian troops were taken prisoner, as well as about 50,000 killed or wounded. The Russian commander, General Alexander Samsonov, committed suicide. The Germans went on to drive Russian forces out of East Prussia, decisively ending the threat of an invasion of Germany from the east.

Far less satisfactory, from a German point of view, was the performance of its ally Austria-Hungary. The first attempt by the Austro-Hungarian army to invade Serbia – the almost forgotten

TURNING POINT

The taxis of the Marne

On 3 September 1914, General Joseph Galliéni, commander of French troops in Paris, was anxiously preparing to defend the city against the advancing German First Army. He learned by reports from reconnaissance aircraft, however, that the Germans had turned southward to pass east of Paris. The following day, Galliéni launched a bold attack on the flank of the German army near the River Marne. It was a desperate venture. At one point, lacking transport, troops were rushed from Paris to the battlefield in taxis. But the surprise attack turned the tide of the war. Other Allied troops also counter-attacked and forced the Germans to retreat. Paris was saved.

pretext for the whole conflict – proved a costly failure. Battle-hardened through their experience in the Balkan Wars, the Serb troops were more than a match for the invaders. In Galicia, clashes between Austro-Hungarian and Russian forces soon went in favour of the Russians, who captured the city of Lemberg (Lvov) in early September. Germany was forced to transfer troops southwards from East Prussia to support the Austro-Hungarians.

French soldiers prepare to use a captured German machine gun during the Battle of the Marne in September 1914. One of the main difficulties the Allied troops had at this stage of the war was a desperate shortage of machine guns of their own.

Meanwhile, on the Western Front, the run of German successes came to an end in the first week of September. According to the Schlieffen Plan, the German armies sweeping down from Belgium were supposed to advance behind the French armies facing the German border. The French would be encircled and destroyed. But the German victory in Lorraine had driven the French back from the frontier zone, making encirclement more difficult. Also, the long march through Belgium and northern France had exhausted German troops and stretched their lines of supply – all supplies having to be carried by horsedrawn vehicles. The Germans swung to the east of Paris, instead of to the west of the city as originally planned, partly to reduce the distance they had to travel. East of Paris, the French and British counter-attacked at the Battle of the Marne.

On 9 September, the German high command ordered its forces to retreat northwards. The Allies set off in pursuit, scenting a chance of victory. When the Germans reached the River Aisne, however, they dug trenches and held their ground. The British and French were incapable of breaking through this defensive position.

Race to the Sea

There was still a large area of open country between the Aisne and the Channel coast which was under no one's control. From September through to November, the Germans and the Allies made a series of attempts to outflank one another in this area, drawing ever closer to the coast. This 'Race to the Sea' resulted in a number of extremely costly battles as each successive outflanking move was blocked. The last of these battles, occurring near the Belgian town of Ypres from 19 October to 22 November, is estimated to have cost a quarter of a million British, French and German casualties.

Cavalry from Algeria (then a French colony) take a rest after fighting at the Battle of the Aisne in September 1914. Soldiers from Africa and Asia played an important part in the conflict.

From mid-November, the onset of winter brought an end to the 'war of movement'. The two sides dug themselves into trenches, facing one another along a front line that stretched unbroken from the English Channel in the north to the border of neutral Switzerland in the south. On the Eastern Front a stable, if looser, line was held as Christmas approached. The human cost of the fighting in 1914 had been unprecedented. France and Germany combined were grieving for over half a million young men killed. Around a third of the British troops sent to France in August had died. Russia and Austria-Hungary had each lost well over a million soldiers dead, wounded or taken prisoner. Yet the fighting had had no decisive result, except to prove how difficult it was going to be for either side to achieve victory.

All armies in the First World War depended heavily on horsedrawn vehicles. This is one reason why decisive, rapid offensives were so hard to carry out. Here, the Bulgarian Army prepares to move up the front line in October 1915.

HOW DID IT HAPPEN?

Could Germany have won the war in 1914?

People have long debated whether, by implementing the original Schlieffen Plan properly, the Germans could have defeated France in August to September 1914. The plan called for German strength to be concentrated on the advance down from Belgium, which was intended to encircle and destroy the French. But German commander, Field Marshal Helmuth von Moltke, weakened these forces, especially by transferring two corps to fight Russia on the Eastern Front.

It has been questioned, however, whether the Schlieffen Plan could ever have succeeded. It required German troops to advance on foot 25 miles a day and fight at the end of ever-lengthening supply lines. Under any circumstances, the exhausted Germans would have become increasingly vulnerable to a counter-attack.

3 Stalemate

The fighting of 1914 left Germany in possession of part of northern France – a valuable area with many factories and mines – and most of Belgium. Britain and France began 1915 determined to drive the Germans out of this territory. But, when they attempted renewed large-scale offensives, they found they could make no progress. Battles such as Neuve Chapelle in March 1915, and Loos in September produced nothing but heavy casualties.

French soldiers in trenches in 1915 wear an early form of gas mask. Goggles cover their eyes and pads soaked in protective chemicals cover their mouths.

The front line from the English Channel to Switzerland remained unchanged throughout the year, except in minor detail.

The reason for the stalemate on the Western Front was the dominance of defence over attack. On both sides, armies dug systems of trenches to protect themselves against enemy fire. Barbed wire was set out in front of the trench. Attackers had to climb out of their trenches and cross no-man's-land under fire from accurate rifles, machine-guns and artillery. They then had to pass through the barbed

VOICES FROM THE PAST

Death by gassing

Poison gas was first used by the Germans at Ypres in April 1915. Six days after the first gas attack, British general, John Charteris, wrote in his diary:

'The horrible part of it is the slow lingering death of those who are gassed. I saw some hundred poor fellows laid out in the open ... slowly drowning with water in their lungs.'

H. P. Willmott, *First World War* (Dorling Kindersly, 2003)

wire to occupy the enemy trench. The defenders would sometimes have a second trench behind the first, so the whole process then had to be repeated. Even if an attacking force managed a momentary breakthrough, it lacked the mobility to advance swiftly through the hole it had made, and the defenders were able to bring up reserves to plug the gap.

Artillery bombardment was used to soften up enemy defences before an attack, but the shells had only limited effect against well-entrenched troops. At the second battle of Ypres in April 1915, the Germans made the first use of poison gas in an attempt to disrupt defences, at first with some success. Gas was soon extensively used by the Allies as well, but the development of counter-measures such as gas masks quickly limited its effectiveness on either side. In the end, the resort to chemical warfare made the battlefield even more dangerous and fearful, but had no decisive effect.

With millions of working men enrolled in the army, Britain was forced to employ women in armaments factories. This sort of work was previously done exclusively by men, and was exhausting and dangerous.

On the Eastern Front, warfare was more mobile than in the west, because there was always room to manoeuvre in the vast spaces over which armies operated. The Russians fared badly during 1915, retreating in the face of a combined German and Austro-Hungarian offensive in the summer. Yet there was no more immediate chance of a decisive victory in the east than in the west.

The combatant countries faced the prospect of a long conflict, in which success would require the massive commitment of industrial production and manpower. By the start of 1915, all the armies were already running short of munitions, especially artillery shells. Countries realized that they needed to organize their industries to maximum effect to support the war effort, while at the same time recruiting the largest possible number of men for the fighting. Britain held out for a long time against the need to introduce conscription. Around 2.5 million British citizens joined the army as volunteers in 1914–16 – almost as many as the army could accommodate. Britain could also draw on troops from its empire and dominions. Canada, Australia, New Zealand and India in particular provided large forces of fighting men. But even in Britain, conscription was finally introduced in 1916.

Soldiers from the Indian subcontinent – then ruled by Britain – fought bravely on the Western Front in 1914 and 1915. They suffered heavy casualties, and were withdrawn from Europe from 1915 onwards.

Civilians rarely became the direct targets of military action, although a small number of air raids were carried out on cities as German zeppelin airships attacked London from 1915 onwards. But civilians were nonetheless profoundly affected by the war. To replace the millions of men being sent to the front, women were drawn into jobs formerly done exclusively by men – from driving buses to working in armaments factories. There were increasing shortages of essential goods, including staple foods, which led to hunger and unrest in many European cities.

Britain and France were better placed than their enemies for a long war, because they could import supplies by sea from around the world, including food and raw materials. The United States was an especially important supplier. Germany tried to cut off these supplies

TURNING POINT

Sinking of the *Lusitania*

On 7 May 1915, the ocean liner *Lusitania*, one of the world's largest and most luxurious passenger ships, was hit by a torpedo fired by a German submarine. The *Lusitania* sank in 18 minutes, drowning more than 1200 passengers and crew. The liner had been sailing from New York to Liverpool, and 128 of the drowned passengers were Americans. The Germans claimed that the liner had been carrying troops and war material but, in fact, it had only a small quantity of ammunition on board. The attack caused anti-German riots in Britain, and outraged American public opinion. Shortly afterwards, Germany had to scale down U-boat activity to avoid war with the United States.

German U-boats line up in Kiel Harbour during the First World War. The use of submarines to attack merchant shipping ultimately played a major part in bringing the United States into the war against Germany.

by using submarines – the U-boats – to sink merchant ships bound for Britain. But the U-boat campaign had to be limited from mid-1915, after the United States threatened to enter the war if attacks on American ships continued.

The surface warships of Britain's Royal Navy, meanwhile, imposed a highly effective blockade that prevented food and raw materials for industry from being imported by the Central Powers.

The rival navies of Britain and Germany fought only one major sea battle, at Jutland in May to June 1916. Although the Royal Navy lost more ships than the Germans, the battle confirmed British domination of the sea, and the German fleet never left port again in the course of the war.

As the war went on, more countries were drawn into the conflict. Italy joined the war on the Allied side in May 1915, after the Allies secretly agreed that the Italians could seize territory from Austria-Hungary if victory was won. In the summer of 1915, Bulgaria joined Germany and Austria-Hungary in an offensive in the Balkans which at last broke Serbian resistance. Serbia was occupied and the remnants of the Serbian army escaped into exile.

Further afield, Japan declared war on Germany and took the opportunity to snap up German possessions in China and the Pacific. Germany's colonies in Africa were attacked by troops from the British dominion of South Africa.

Heavy artillery, such as this Italian howitzer, was used by all sides in the war to rain down massive quantities of explosives upon enemy trenches. This sort of heavy shelling, however, repeatedly failed to lead to any decisive breakthrough in trench warfare.

But by far the most important geographical widening of the conflict resulted from the Ottoman Empire (Turkey) entering the war on the German side in November 1914. Because the Turks ruled an area stretching from the Mediterranean to Mesopotamia, their entry into the war led to far-reaching consequences for the entire Middle East.

Faced with stalemate on the Western Front, in the spring of 1915, Britain decided to attempt to capture the Ottoman capital, Constantinople (Istanbul), thus opening up a sea route to provide military aid to Russia. A large military force, including many Australians and New Zealanders, landed on the Turkish coast at Gallipoli in April, in order to seize control of the straits that led to Constantinople. But the troops met fierce resistance from the Turkish army, and lost some 250,000 men killed or wounded before the operation was finally abandoned in January 1916.

HOW DID IT HAPPEN?

Why did men go on fighting?

Historians have debated why troops kept on fighting despite the terrible conditions under which the war was fought and heavy casualties. One obvious reason was what military historian Keith Simpson called 'fear of the consequences of disobedience'. For example, 346 British soldiers were executed for refusing to fight. There was also a strong sense of solidarity with comrades in arms – soliders did not want to let their friends down. Patriotism was a further powerful motive – they felt it was their duty to win the war on their country's behalf. British war correspondent, Phillip Gibbs, wrote of men on opposing sides being driven by 'a deep and simple love of England [or] Germany.'

But historian Niall Ferguson has asserted that an instinctive love of fighting and killing also played its part, writing: 'Men kept fighting because they wanted to.' He quotes a Canadian soldier who described the war as 'the greatest adventure of my life ... I would not have missed it for anything.'

Keith Simpson quoted in Richard Holmes, *The Western Front*, (BBC, 1999); Philip Gibbs quoted in H. P. Willmott, *First World War* (Dorling Kindersley, 2003); Niall Ferguson, *The Pity of War* (Penguin, 1998)

An Australian soldier carries a wounded comrade during the fighting at Gallipoli in 1915. About 11,000 of the 48,000 Allied soldiers killed in the Gallipoli campaign were from Australia or New Zealand.

Elsewhere in the Ottoman Empire, the British fought the Turks with mixed success in Mesopotamia, and supported a revolt against Turkish rule by Arabs in what is now Saudi Arabia – an operation in which T. E. Lawrence ('Lawrence of Arabia') played a significant part. For their part, the Turks invaded the Caucasus region of Russia in the winter of 1914–15, only to be driven back with heavy losses. The worst consequence of the war with Russia was felt by the Armenians, more than 2 million of whom

lived under Turkish rule. Suspecting the Armenians of co-operating with the Russians, the Turkish government had the whole population deported. Around 1.5 million Armenians died of hardship and massacre between 1915 and 1917. Wherever the war spread its tentacles, it brought death and suffering on an awesome scale.

4 Near Breaking Point

Despite the widening of the conflict to other parts of the world, the combatant countries remained certain that the war would be won or lost on the major battlefields of Europe. After a year of frustration in 1915, they prepared for even mightier offensives in 1916, ready to use the now much greater quantity of arms and ammunition being supplied by their war industries.

At a conference held at Chantilly, France, in December 1915, the British, French, Italians and Russians agreed on a plan to mount simultaneous offensives so that the Central Powers would have to fight on all fronts at once. But the Germans had their own attacking plans. General Erich von Falkenhayn, who had taken over from Moltke as German Chief of General Staff, decided to concentrate his forces against the French fortress city of Verdun. He believed that the French would feel obliged to defend Verdun at any cost. It would become a killing ground on which, Falkenhayn wrote, 'the forces of France will bleed to death'.

VOICES FROM THE PAST

Annihilation

German soldiers suffered as heavily in the battles of 1916 as the British and French. Lieutenant Ernst Jünger described the German lines in September 1916:

'The sunken road now appeared as nothing but a series of enormous shell-holes filled with pieces of uniform, weapons and dead bodies ... Among the living lay the dead. As we dug ourselves in we found them in layers stacked one on top of the other. One company after another had been shoved into the drum-fire [machine-gun fire] and steadily annihilated.'

Ernst Jünger, *Storm of Steel* (Penguin, 2004)

The Germans launched their offensive against Verdun on 21 February 1916, with the heaviest artillery bombardment the world had yet seen. As Falkenhayn had guessed, the French government decreed that Verdun must be held at whatever cost. General Philippe Pétain was put in command of the defence of the city, and hundreds of thousands of French troops were funnelled into that small sector of the front. A single road, soon known to the French as the *voie sacrée* (sacred way), linked Verdun to the rear. Although the road was under continual artillery bombardment, around 3000 trucks travelled along it every day, carrying men and supplies to the battlefield.

Falkenhayn had anticipated that the French troops would simply be worn down by artillery fire, keeping German casualties to a minimum. But the German troops were increasingly drawn into fierce combat, some of it at close quarters in and around the old forts that had been built to defend Verdun. By the time the offensive was called off in early June, the Germans had suffered over 280,000 casualties – only slightly less less than the 315,000 French dead or wounded. And for all their efforts, the Germans still failed to take Verdun, allowing France to claim a victory.

At the Chantilly conference, the British and French had agreed to launch a joint offensive on the section of the Western Front near the

French troops crouch down as artillery shells explode in front of them during the Battle of Verdun in 1916. At the start of the battle, the German guns fired over a million shells in a single day.

River Somme in the summer of 1916. The French losses at Verdun so weakened France's army, however, that it had limited resources left to throw into a new offensive. The British army, on the other hand, had been growing rapidly in size as volunteers joined up in their hundreds of thousands. So the Somme offensive became a largely British operation, under the command of Field Marshal Sir Douglas Haig.

British machine-gunners in gas masks take part in the Battle of the Somme in 1916. The use of machine guns by both sides meant that troops advancing towards enemy trenches were mown down in their thousands.

Haig believed that a prolonged artillery bombardment, backed up by the exploding of mines in tunnels dug under the German lines, would break German resistance. Infantry would advance to occupy the devastated German trenches and cavalry would ride through into open country behind the German lines. But the disastrous first day of the battle, on 1 July, proved the artillery was nowhere near as effective as Haig expected. The following months reinforced this lesson. Despite attack after attack by Allied infantry, the German lines barely moved. Beaumont-Hamel, for example, was one of the objectives that the British intended to seize on 1 July; they actually took it on 13 November, the day the offensive was finally called off.

TURNING POINT

First day of the Somme

On 1 July 1916, the British Army, along with a lesser number of
French troops, launched a major offensive on the Somme.
In the eight days before the offensive, over a million artillery
shells were fired at the German trenches. This bombardment
was expected to crush German resistance. British infantry –
mostly new troops entering their first battle – were ordered to
advance at walking pace across no-man's-land to occupy the
German lines. But as the troops advanced, the Germans
emerged unscathed from their deep shelters and opened fire.
The shelling had also failed to clear away the barbed wire in
front of the German trenches. Unable to advance, and caught in
machine-gun fire, line after line of British soldiers were mown
down. Of 100,000 men who attacked that day, almost 20,000
were killed and another 40,000 were wounded or missing.

Around 600,000 Allied troops were killed or wounded in the
battle of the Somme. Estimates of German casualties vary, but they
were almost certainly on a similar scale. Overshadowed by this
immense slaughter were a few positive developments. A newly
created British mass army began to find out how to fight – a painful
and expensive learning process, but learning nonetheless. Also, new
weapons were introduced that could potentially break the deadlock.
The British used tanks for the first time at the Somme, although there
were too few of them, and they were too slow and unreliable to have
much effect. Aircraft had begun to play an important part in the war
– employed chiefly as 'eyes in the sky' – directing artillery fire on
to enemy targets. But the planes were not yet very effective as
bombers, or for attacking troops on the ground. For the time being,
increasing supplies of arms and munitions simply increased the toll of
dead and wounded.

The Pressure Mounts

On the Eastern Front, in 1916, there was once again more movement
than in the west, but mass slaughter on a similar scale. In the spring,
the Russians launched an offensive in Poland. Their troops
outnumbered the Germans by six to one, yet the Russians were driven
back with heavy losses. In June, however, Russian General Alexei

Brusilov launched a successful offensive against Austro-Hungarian forces in Galicia. Attacking without a preparatory artillery bombardment, his troops took the Austro-Hungarians by surprise and drove them back in disarray, taking more than 300,000 prisoners. Germany was forced to transfer troops from the Western Front to counter-attack against the Russians. Despite the initial success, Russia eventually lost around a million men in the Brusilov offensive – killed, wounded or taken prisoner – for little ultimate gain.

Battered by the Russian offensive, and also engaging the Italians in the south, the Austro-Hungarian army was almost spent by the summer of 1916. Germany had to take command of its ally's military forces to keep them fighting. The effectiveness of this move was shown when Romania declared war on the Central Powers in August, 1916, hoping to take advantage of Austria-Hungary's weakness to seize territory from Hungary. Romania was soon invaded by armies under German command, and its capital, Bucharest, fell to the Central Powers in December.

David Lloyd George (right), British prime minister from December 1916 to the end of the war, talks to French commander, General Joseph Joffre (centre) and British commander, Field Marshal Sir Douglas Haig.

HOW DID IT HAPPEN?

Lions led by donkeys?

The troops in the trenches have been described as 'lions led by donkeys' – courageous men sent to their deaths in futile offensives by generals who were insensitive, unimaginative fools. Historian A. J. P. Taylor summed up this view of the war as: 'brave helpless soldiers; blundering obstinate generals; nothing achieved.'

But other historians have argued that the generals fought the war in the only way it could be fought, at a time when artillery, machine guns and barbed wire dominated the battlefield. Historian John Keegan wrote: 'The basic and stark fact ... was that the conditions of warfare between 1914 and 1918 predisposed towards slaughter and that only an entirely different technology, one not available until a generation later, could have averted such an outcome.'

A. J. P. Taylor, *The First World War* (Penguin, 1963); John Keegan, *The First World War* (Hutchinson, 1998)

General Alexei Brusilov was the most successful Russian general of the war, inflicting a severe setback upon Austria-Hungary with his offensive in the summer of 1916. But even Brusilov was not able to achieve a decisive victory and his offensive ultimately cost Russia many men.

The massive scale of losses at the front, and lack of prospect of an end to the war, put immense strain on people's loyalty to their governments. So did the mounting hardship among civilians, especially where food shortages became serious, as in Austria-Hungary and Russia. Austria-Hungary faced particular problems because the loyalty of the different nationalities within the empire weakened as the war went on. There were, for example, large-scale desertions by Czech troops from the Austro-Hungarian army during 1916. Britain faced its own nationalist problem in Ireland, where Republicans seeking independence from British rule staged an uprising in Dublin in Easter 1916, hoping for German support that never came. The uprising was repressed by the British army in a brutal manner that turned many more Irish people against British rule.

In Russia, the Tsarist regime had reached breaking point by the end of the year, and was on the brink of a revolution that would change the course of world history.

5 America Joins the War

B y the end of 1916, the Central Powers were pessimistic about the future of the war. The German government made an offer of peace to the Allies, based on Germany keeping possession of the territory it currently held – a proposal totally unacceptable to the Allied powers. After the peace offer had been rejected, Germany's leaders decided upon a desperate gamble. They would resume unlimited U-boat warfare, hoping to sink enough merchant ships to bring Britain to its knees. The Germans knew that the United States would probably enter the war if its merchant ships were sunk, but gambled that the war could be won before American manpower and industrial might could have any effect on the European battlefield.

Believing that the U-boats could win the war, the Germans decided to use a defensive strategy on the Western Front. In early 1917, German troops were withdrawn to newly constructed fortified positions along what was known as the Hindenburg Line. The Allies, by contrast, continued to have confidence in attack. A charismatic general, Robert Nivelle, took over from Marshal Joseph Joffre as French commander-in-chief, and promised to 'win the war in 48 hours' with a single, concentrated offensive. Launched in April 1917, the Nivelle offensive proved an utter disaster. The Allies lost around 350,000 men for almost no gain. In the wake of the offensive there were widespread mutinies in the French army. Nivelle was dismissed and replaced by Pétain, who restored order in the ranks with a mixture of firmness and concessions. But the spirit of the French army was broken.

French deserters make their way towards German lines to surrender to the enemy. In April to May 1917, many French soldiers refused to obey orders and organized protests against their officers. However, few actually deserted, and morale was gradually restored.

Allied offensives on the Western Front, with British and Commonwealth forces playing the leading role, continued through the year. The fighting at Ypres in July to November, which became known as the battle of Passchendaele, was perhaps the most hellish of the war. Some soldiers simply drowned in the mud as constant rainfall

French soldiers captured by the Germans during the disasterous Nivelle Offensive of spring 1917, are taken away to a prisoner of war camp. In general, prisoners of war on both sides on the Western Front were reasonably well treated.

VOICES FROM THE PAST

A call for peace

Siegfried Sassoon, a British poet and army officer with a record of exceptional bravery, decided in 1917 that the war must be ended. He issued a public appeal for peace:

'I believe that the war is being deliberately prolonged by those who have the power to end it ... I have seen and endured the suffering of the troops, and I can no longer be a party to prolong these sufferings for ends which I believe to be evil and unjust.'

Sassoon's peace appeal was dismissed by the authorities as the product of shell shock and he was sent to a military hospital.

Jon Stallworthy, *Wilfred Owen: A Biography* (OUP, 1975)

Canadian soldiers use shell holes to provide cover during the fighting at Passchendaele in 1917. The conditions at Passchendaele were terrible, with mud sometimes so deep that men who slipped into it sank without trace.

reduced the battlefield to a swamp. As usual, Allied advances of a few hundred metres were bought with tens of thousands of casualties. Meanwhile, in Italy, German and Austro-Hungarian forces managed a breakthrough at Caporetto in October, forcing Britain and France to transfer resources to the Italian front to prevent their ally from being defeated.

The Collapse of Russia

If 1917 was a year of continuing stalemate on the Western Front, on the Eastern Front it brought dramatic changes. In Russia, the Tsarist regime collapsed under the strain of the war. Tsar Nicholas II was forced to abdicate in March after a popular uprising provoked by food shortages in the capital, Petrograd (St Petersburg). A provisional government took over, dedicated to continuing the war. The strongest figure in the new government was Alexander Kerensky. In the summer of 1917, Kerensky ordered a major offensive to drive the enemy from Russian soil. It proved a costly failure.

Meanwhile, anti-war feeling in Russia was mounting. Russian revolutionary, Vladimir Ilyich Lenin, the leader of the Bolshevik party, was in exile in Switzerland when the Tsarist regime fell. In April,

Lenin accepted a German offer of transport back to his homeland, crossing Germany in a sealed train. As the Germans had hoped, Lenin led agitation for an immediate end to the war and a further, more extreme revolution. His slogan was: 'Bread, Peace and Land'.

After the failure of the Kerensky offensive, the Russian army began to fall apart. Soldiers deserted in their thousands, or formed revolutionary committees and ignored orders from their officers. In Petrograd, a complex political struggle ended in November when the Bolsheviks overthrew the provisional government and set up their own revolutionary government with Lenin at its head. Lenin immediately issued a proclamation advocating a 'just and democratic peace', and calling on the people in all combatant countries to revolt against their rulers and end the war. On 15 December, the Bolsheviks signed an armistice with the Germans and opened peace negotiations.

The collapse of Russia was a great boost for the Germans, but it was a triumph that they desperately needed for, by this time, the United States had entered the war against them. The resumption of unlimited U-boat warfare in February 1917 was a direct challenge to the United States, since many of the ships sunk on their way to British ports would inevitably be American. The Zimmermann telegram (see panel), was also interpreted by most Americans as a hostile act.

Bolshivik leader Vladimir Ilyich Lenin addresses a crowd in Petrograd (St Petersburg) during the Russian Revolution. Standing alongside the podium, on the right of the picture, is another leading revolutionary, Leon Trotsky.

TURNING POINT

Zimmermann telegram

On 17 January 1917, the German foreign minister, Arthur Zimmermann, sent the German ambassador in Mexico a proposal for an alliance between Germany and Mexico. The Mexicans were to be encouraged 'to reconquer the lost territory in Texas, New Mexico and Arizona' from the United States. Zimmermann did not know that both British and American intelligence services were eavesdropping on transatlantic communications. They intercepted the message. In early March, the content of the telegram was revealed to the American public. It caused a sensation, turning American opinion decisively against Germany.

US President Woodrow Wilson saw himself as a man of peace. He had been re-elected in 1916 with the slogan: 'He kept us out of the war.' But, on 2 April, he asked Congress to authorize a declaration of war on Germany, saying: 'The world must be made safe for democracy.' America entered the war on 6 April, although it tried to keep its distance from Britain and France. Instead of joining the Allies, the United States became only an 'Associate Power'.

Representatives of the Russian Bolshevik government, and of Germany and its allies, meet at Brest-Litovsk to sign an armistice. The harsh peace terms imposed on Russia at Brest-Litovsk in March 1918, deprived the country of more than a third of its pre-war population.

The U-boat campaign at first threatened to achieve all that the Germans had hoped. In April 1917, one in four ships sailing to Britain was sunk. The imports on which Britain depended to survive were being cut off. And American troops could never be shipped across to Europe if losses were occurring on such a scale. But, in May, Britain introduced a convoy system. Merchant ships crossed the Atlantic in large groups under naval protection. The result was a drop in losses from around 25 percent to 1 percent. The British government was still forced to ration many imported foodstuffs in short supply, but Britain could go on fighting.

The United States had only a small peacetime army. Training and equipping an army to fight in Europe was a slow process, so the Americans had no immediate impact on the fighting. But the entry of the United States into the war and the fall of the Tsar in Russia

HOW DID IT HAPPEN?

Why did America join in the European war?

US President Woodrow Wilson presented America's entry into the war as an act of idealism. He claimed that the United States had no selfish motive – not even 'to defend our territory' – but was acting as 'the champion of right and liberty'.

But some historians have challenged this idealistic view of American action, arguing that the United States exploited the opportunity presented by the war to increase its economic and political power. Specifically, providing Britain and France with supplies had become vital to the American economy. Americans had also lent the Allies very large sums of money to pay for these supplies. The United States had to ensure that the Allies did not lose the war, or the loans would never be repaid and the US economy would suffer.

Other historians have argued that German domination of Europe would have been a long-term threat to American security and therefore had to be resisted. However, no one has produced any documentary evidence to show that Wilson had other than idealistic motives.

American soldiers about to set off on the long journey to Europe say farewell to their families. More than 2 million 'doughboys' eventually crossed the Atlantic, giving a massive boost to the Allied war effort.

together had a profound effect on war aims. The Allies were now able to present their war as a struggle for democracy, freedom and national self-determination – the right of national groups to govern themselves. This had not been possible while the Tsarist regime – an enemy of democracy and ruler of many nations within its empire – was an ally.

The changing situation also encouraged anti-war feeling in Germany. For many Germans, the main motive for supporting the war had been fear of conquest by Tsarist Russia. With the threat of the Tsar gone, in July 1917, the German Reichstag (parliament) voted in favour of a 'peace resolution'. But the Reichstag did not have control over the German High Command. Encouraged by the collapse of Russia, in November 1917, Ludendorff and his colleagues decided that, in the following spring, they would launch a final colossal offensive on the Western Front. They believed that they could win the war in 1918.

6 The Final Battles

On 3 March 1918, the Russian Bolshevik government signed a peace treaty with the Germans at Brest-Litovsk. It was a humiliating agreement that the Bolsheviks only agreed to sign because the Russian army had dissolved and they were defenceless against German military might. Russia was forced to accept the loss of two-fifths of the population of the former Russian Empire: Poland, Ukraine, Belorus, Finland, Moldova, the Baltic states of Lithuania, Latvia and Estonia, and Armenia, Azerbaijan and Georgia all became independent, at least in principle. In practice, they were subject to strict control and ruthless economic exploitation by Germany and Austria-Hungary.

Dead British soldiers lie in a trench captured by the Germans in the offensive of spring 1918. Initially a triumph for Germany, the offensive eventually exhausted the German Army and exposed it to counter-attack.

VOICES FROM THE PAST

Fight to a finish

In April 1918, British military leaders seriously feared that their army might be facing defeat. The British commander, Field Marshal Douglas Haig, issued a ringing proclamation to his troops, who were bearing the weight of the German offensive:

'With our backs to the wall and believing in the justice of our cause, each one of us must fight to the end ... Every position must be held to the last man.'

Quoted in John Keegan, *The First World War* (Hutchinson 1998)

The harsh terms imposed on Russia convinced even many Germans that Germany's rulers were fighting a war of conquest, not of self-defence. There was a wave of strikes in German and Austro-Hungarian factories by workers who sympathized with the Bolsheviks and demanded a just peace.

For the German High Command, however, the triumph in the east presented the opportunity to transfer troops to reinforce the Western Front. The Germans knew that they had to exploit the advantage this gave them quickly – before American soldiers began to arrive in Europe in large numbers. On 21 March 1918, masses of German troops supported by over 10,000 artillery guns and mortars launched an offensive against the British armies on the Somme. Known as the Michael Offensive or the *Kaiserschlacht* (Kaiser's battle), it was initially an overwhelming success. The British lines were ripped apart. The long stalemate on the Western Front was at an end. Follow-up offensives in April and May carried the Germans to within less than 100 kilometres of Paris.

As early as 23 March, a triumphant Kaiser Wilhelm granted all German schoolchildren a holiday to celebrate 'Victory Day'. Yet, after initial panic, the Allies rallied in the face of the overwhelming onslaught. For the first time in the war, British and French forces were joined under a single commander-in-chief, French General Ferdinand Foch. Despite their gains of territory, the Germans suffered heavy losses – 348,000 in the first six weeks of the offensive. The Allies also lost hundreds of

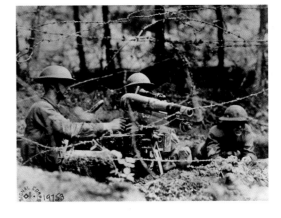

American soldiers fight on the Western Front. The arrival of the 'doughboys' meant that, despite the heavy casualties suffered by Britain and France in the battles of spring and summer 1918, the number of troops on the Allied side continued to grow.

thousands of men, but enough American 'doughboys' – the nickname for the American infantry – were arriving in Europe to replace them. About 200,000 US troops landed in France in the month of May alone. Commanded by General John Pershing, they fought their first action against the Germans at Chateau-Thierry on the Marne in early June.

French tanks advance towards the war zone in 1918. The large-scale use of tanks by the Allies in 1918 helped break the stalemate.

Through the early summer, the Germans continued to attack, but with diminishing success. By August, the Allies were ready to launch a counter-offensive. On 8 August, Canadian and Australian infantry, supported by 350 tanks and over 2,000 aircraft, attacked at Amiens, pushing the Germans back and inflicting heavy casualties. Ludendorff called it 'the black day of the German army'. Two days later he told the Kaiser that Germany could no longer hope to win the war.

Through the following months, the Allies launched a series of successful offensives that, by early October, had carried them beyond the Hindenburg Line into territory the Germans had held since 1914. The Allies were far superior to the Germans in the use of tanks, which had now developed into a major force on the battlefield, and their planes dominated the air, bombing and strafing German soldiers and supply lines. The freshness of the American troops also contributed to the Allied success, although their inexperience meant they often suffered especially heavy casualties. The Germans, meanwhile, worn down by years of fighting and demoralized by the failure of their spring offensive to win the war, began to surrender in increasing numbers.

The Central Powers Collapse

Away from the Western Front, Germany's allies were crumbling. In the Ottoman Empire, the British had captured Jerusalem in December 1917 and, in September 1918, decisively defeated Turkish forces at the Battle of Megiddo. On the Italian front, the Austro-Hungarian army was in disarray after a last failed offensive in the summer of 1918. In the Balkans, an Allied army, advancing north from the Greek port of Salonika, attacked Bulgaria on 15 September. The Bulgarians surrendered within two weeks.

On 29 September, Ludendorff told the Kaiser that Germany must seek an immediate end to the fighting. There were as yet no foreign troops on

General John Pershing (left) was the commander of American forces in Europe. He did not agree with President Wilson's desire for a compromise peace, instead arguing for a total military victory and for the imposition of harsh terms on Germany.

TURNING POINT

Wilson's 14 points

On 8 January 1918, President Wilson announced a 14-point plan for a just peace. Some of the points were proposals for a better post-war world. For example, general disarmament would cut all countries' arms to the minimum required for national defence, and an international organization would be set up to guarantee countries against attack by their neighbours. Other points were more specific. Germany was to hand back territory occupied during the war, as well as Alsace-Lorraine. Poland – previously divided up between Germany, Austria-Hungary and Russia – was to become an independent state. National groups in the Austro-Hungarian and Ottoman Empires were to be given autonomy – not full independence, but a large say in running their own affairs. The existence of Wilson's peace plan became a major factor in ending the war in the autumn of 1918.

British troops formally occupy Jerusalem, Palestine, in December 1917. Palestine had been ruled by the Turks as part of the Ottoman Empire, but after the war it came under British administration.

German soil, and the German line on the Western Front was unbroken. The German leaders hoped that they could still make a deal that would enable them to claim to be undefeated. On 4 October, they told Wilson that they accepted his 14-point peace plan, and asked him to arrange a ceasefire.

By negotiating with Wilson, the German leaders hoped to get lenient terms. But the British and French, as well as American military leaders, made certain that an armistice was offered only on tough conditions, designed to ensure that the Germans could not start fighting again at a later date. German territory west of the Rhine was to be occupied by Allied forces, and large quantities of Germany military equipment were to be handed over to the Allies. Some German military leaders, including Ludendorff, wanted to reject these terms and fight on. But the Kaiser dismissed Ludendorff on 26 October.

HOW DID IT HAPPEN?

Why did Germany lose?

Many British military historians believe that the war was won primarily because the British army learned to combine infantry, artillery, tanks and planes in a modern style of warfare that was simply too good for the Germans. Other historians have highlighted the overwhelming importance of the arrival of hundreds of thousands of fresh American troops in the summer of 1918. This contributed to what historian Niall Ferguson called 'a crisis of German morale', which saw around 360,000 German soldiers surrender in the last three months of the war.

By contrast, after the war, many Germans held the view that their army had never been defeated on the battlefield at all. Ludendorff in particular claimed that the German army had been 'stabbed in the back' by politically motivated groups at home who undermined the war effort. But historian A. J. P. Taylor countered that losing the war caused a revolution, not the other way round: 'The German revolution … was caused by Ludendorff's confession that the war was lost.'

Niall Ferguson, *The Pity of War* (Penguin, 1998); A. J. P. Taylor, *The First World War* (Penguin, 1963)

In practice, the worsening political situation inside Germany made continuing the war an impossible option. The German people were suffering dire hardship. Largely as a result of the British naval blockade, there were chronic shortages of food and fuel. The country was seething with unrest. When, outraged by the armistice terms, naval commander Admiral Reinhardt Scheer ordered the German fleet to set sail for a final showdown with the Royal Navy, the sailors refused to obey. Instead, the port of Kiel was taken over by revolutionary sailors and workers. In early November, major cities across Germany fell under revolutionary control.

Austria-Hungary was in even worse condition, because popular unrest similar to that in Germany was accompanied by ethnic divisions. With the encouragement of the Allies, the country's Poles, Czechs and other Slav minorities began organizing their own governments and claiming areas of Austro-Hungarian territory. By the time Austria-Hungary signed an armistice with the Allies on 3 November, the Austro-Hungarian Empire had already effectively ceased to exist.

On 9 November, Germany was proclaimed a republic and the Kaiser abdicated, fleeing to exile in the Netherlands. Two days later – still protesting about the terms they were being forced to accept – a German delegation signed the armistice in a railway carriage in the Forest of Compiègne in eastern France. The guns fell silent on the Western Front at 11 o'clock on 11 November 1918.

This photograph shows recently captured German prisoners of war at Abbeville, France, in August 1918. The fact that German soldiers began to surrender in large numbers indicates how demoralized they had become.

7 A Failed Peace

The announcement of the armistice on 11 November 1918, was greeted by the countries on the winning side with unbridled celebrations. Delirious crowds filled the streets in major cities such as London, Paris, New York, Chicago, and Melbourne. But even among the victors were millions of people in no mood to celebrate – especially those in mourning for brothers, sons, or fathers lost in the war. In much of the rest of the world, defeated and devastated, there was no cause for rejoicing at all.

French people flood onto the Parisian boulevards to celebrate the armistice on 11 November 1918. There were similar scenes in London and other major cities in the countries on the winning side.

No one knows for certain how many people died in the First World War. The total number of men killed in the fighting is estimated at between 8.5 million and 9.8 million. Germany lost over 2 million men on the battlefields, Russia probably 1.8 million, France 1.4 million, Austria-Hungary over a million, Britain and its empire around 900,000, Italy almost half a million and the US 50,000. Those who died in battle were mostly young men. Of German men who were between the ages of 19 and 22 when the war started, one in three died.

The war also took a heavy toll in civilian casualties. According to some estimates, for example, 700,000 German civilians may have died through hardship and malnutrition during the war and in its aftermath, mostly as a result of the British naval blockade which was maintained until June 1919. Some small countries suffered disproportionately. Around 600,000 Serbian civilians and perhaps half a million civilians in Romania are thought to have perished as a result of the effects of the war.

Even more people died as a result of a virulent influenza epidemic which was a by-product of the war. This 'Spanish flu' probably first appeared on the Western Front in the spring of 1918. Spreading worldwide during 1918–9, it killed 20 million people, including 62,000 US soldiers.

The Peace Treaties

In January 1919, the leaders of the victorious powers gathered in Paris for a peace conference. The defeated nations were not invited. Proceedings were dominated by the 'big four': Britain, France, the United States and Italy. US President Wilson aimed to create a new

VOICES FROM THE PAST

'The dead were dead...'

Vera Brittain served as a nurse during the war, in which some of her closest friends and family were killed. On the evening that peace was declared, she went out with some colleagues to mingle with celebrating crowds in central London. She later wrote:

'Wherever we went a burst of enthusiastic cheering greeted our Red Cross uniform, and complete strangers ... rushed up and shook me warmly by the hand ... I detached myself from the others and walked slowly up Whitehall, with my heart sinking in a sudden cold dismay ... The war was over; a new age was beginning; but the dead were dead and would never return.'

Vera Brittain, *Testament of Youth* (Virago, 1978)

At Brookwood Cemetery in Surrey, southern England, people visit the graves of dead soldiers on a memorial day in June 1919. The graves of American soldiers buried in the cemetery have been marked with American flags.

order in Europe based on democracy and self-determination – the redrawing of borders so that each ethnic group could live under its own national government. The French Prime Minister, Georges Clemenceau, by contrast, wanted above all to weaken Germany so that it could not attack France again in the future.

Diplomats look on as the peace treaty with Germany is signed in the Hall of Mirrors at Versailles on 28 June 1919.

A French gunboat keeps watch over the Ruhr river during the occupation of part of Germany in 1923.

Of the series of peace treaties made with the defeated countries, the most important was the Versailles Treaty with Germany. Under its terms, the Germans had to hand back Alsace-Lorraine to France, as well as give up a modest amount of other territory – for example, giving Poland access to the sea by a corridor across German territory to the port of Danzig (Gdansk). The German army was limited to 100,000 men, with no tanks or aircraft. The Germans were to pay 'reparations' to Britain, France, Italy and Belgium to compensate for the damage these countries had suffered. And they had to admit that the war had been a result of German aggression – this was known as the 'war guilt clause'. German representatives signed the peace treaty on 28 June 1919, but only after the Allies had threatened to resume the war and invade Germany.

The peacemakers in Paris had little or no control over most of the changes that resulted from the war. Amid the ruins of the Russian, Austro-Hungarian and Ottoman Empires, competing groups fought to establish new borders and regimes. New states, including Finland, Poland, Czechoslovakia and Yugoslavia, were created by nationalist groups. The borders of the new states were mostly decided by local wars. For example, Poland extended its territory eastward in 1920 by winning a war with Russia.

Inside Russia, civil war raged between the Bolshevik government and its enemies from 1918 to 1920. This immensely destructive conflict ended with the Bolsheviks in control of the majority of the territory of the former Russian Empire, which became the Soviet Union in 1922. There was also warfare in Turkey, where nationalist leader Kemal Ataturk deposed the Ottoman sultan to found a Turkish republic, and defeated an attempt by Greece to take a large slice of Turkish territory. Britain and France between them reorganized the rest of the former Ottoman Empire (the British, among other things, creating the new Arab state of Iraq).

The borders that resulted from the peace conference and from these postwar conflicts did not fulfil Wilson's ideal of national self-determination. For example, Austria was forbidden to unite with Germany, although its population was overwhelmingly German. Wilson's idea for an international organization to

The first meeting of the League of Nations takes place in Geneva in 1920. The failure of the United States to join the new international organization partly undermined its effectiveness from the outset.

VOICES FROM THE PAST

Ripping up the treaty

In April 1939, German dictator, Adolf Hitler, described how his political career had been dedicated to undoing the Versailles Treaty:

'I have ... endeavoured to destroy sheet by sheet the treaty which ... contains the vilest oppression which peoples and human beings have ever been expected to put up with.'

J. Fest, *Hitler* (Weidenfeld & Nicholson, 1973)

maintain peace in the future was, however, adopted. The League of Nations was intended to ensure that all countries would unite against any state that resorted to war. But when Wilson went back to the United States after the peace conference, the US Congress refused to ratify the peace treaty, arguing that belonging to the League of Nations might involve America in future European wars. The failure of the United States to join the League of Nations weakened the organization from the outset.

The First World War left a legacy of discontent and bitterness. The attempt to force Germany to pay reparations, which led to the occupation of the Ruhr district of Germany by France and Belgium in 1923, plagued international relations in Europe. The world economy, disrupted by the war and its aftermath, could not recover its pre-war stability and plunged into the Great Depression in the late 1920s. Germany was especially hard-hit by the Depression, and the mass unemployment that came with it.

Right-wing German nationalists – such as Nazi Party leader, Adolf Hitler – blamed most of his country's misfortunes on the Versailles Treaty. After Hitler came to power in Germany in 1933, neither Britain and France, nor the League of Nations, was prepared to prevent him from rearming Germany and embarking on a policy of armed expansion that led to the Second World War in 1939. Hitler's aim was essentially to reverse the results of the First World War. His defeat of France in 1940 was sealed by a humiliating peace agreement, signed in the same railway carriage used for the signing of the armistice in November 1918.

By 1923, the countries of Europe had settled into a new shape. Germany lost some territory, mostly to Poland and France. Part of Germany – East Prussia – was cut off from the rest of the country by a strip of territory giving Poland access to the sea at Danzig (Gdansk). The break-up of the Austro-Hungarian Empire left Austria as a small country of mostly German population.

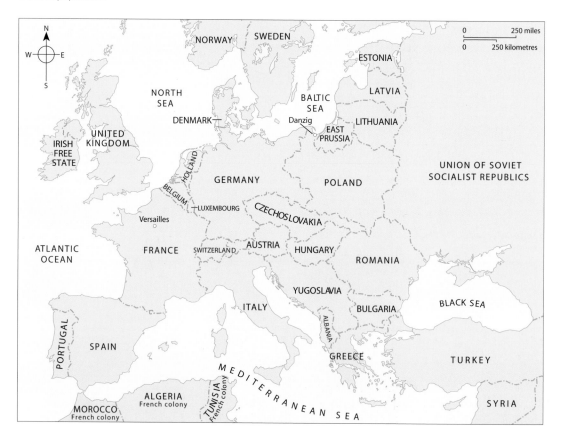

The First World War had utterly failed to be 'the war to end wars', as some had hoped at the time. But it did change attitudes about warfare. When the Second World War started, there were no cheering crowds to be seen in European cities – not even in Nazi Germany. The sacrifice of the millions who died on the Western Front was not forgotten. It is still remembered in annual ceremonies today, even as the last few survivors of those who fought in the war fade away.

Adolf Hitler, the leader of the Nazi Party, had fought in the trenches in the First World War. After coming to power in Germany in 1933 he rebuilt the country's military strength and set out to reverse the result of the war – an ambition that led to an even more devastating global conflict in 1939–45.

HOW DID IT HAPPEN?

Guilt of the peacemakers?

The German delegates who reluctantly signed the Versailles treaty in 1919, protested at 'the unheard of injustice of the conditions of peace'. Whether the peacemakers at Versailles really treated Germany too harshly has been the subject of intense debate. Influential British economist J. M. Keynes thought so at the time. In his 1919 book *The Economic Consequences of the Peace*, he wrote: 'The Peace [Treaty] is outrageous and impossible and can bring nothing but misfortune.'

According to historian Niall Ferguson, however, the peace terms were not especially harsh and 'Germany came out of the war no worse off than Britain, and in some respects better off.' A large number of historians have felt that the treaty, although far from perfect, was probably the best that could have been achieved under the circumstances of the time. A. J. P. Taylor, for example, pointed out that the way the Germans were treated was inevitable, writing: 'A peace of reconciliation' would have meant accepting 'that there was nothing to choose between the two sides and that the only fault of the Germans was to have lost. Who dared say that at the time? Who, outside Germany, would say it now?'

German quote from Martin Gilbert, *A History of the Twentieth Century* (HarperCollins, 1997); J. M. Keynes quoted in Niall Ferguson, *The Pity of War* (Penguin, 1998); A. J. P. Taylor, *The First World War* (Penguin, 1963)

First World War Timeline

1914

28 June: Assassination of Austrian Archduke Franz Ferdinand

July: Austria-Hungary declares war on Serbia

1 August: Germany declares war on Russia

3 August: Germany declares war on France

4 August: Britain declares war on Germany

23 August: British encounter German forces at Mons

26–30 August: Battle of Tannenberg

6 September: Beginning of the First Battle of the Marne

16 November: The Ottoman Empire enters the war on the side of the Central Powers

22 November: The First Battle of Ypres ends in stalemate

1915

25 April: Allied forces land at Gallipoli, Turkey

7 May: The *Lusitania* is sunk by a German U-boat

23 May: Italy enters the war on the Allied side

July to August: Russian forces withdraw from Poland

October: Bulgaria allies itself with Central Powers

October to November: Central Powers occupy Serbia

19 December: Allied troops begin evacuation from Gallipoli

1916

21 February: The Germans launch a massive offensive against the French at Verdun

31 May: Battle of Jutland

June to July: The Brusilov offensive

June: Arabs revolt against Ottoman rule

1 July: Beginning of the Battle of the Somme

August to December: Romania enters the war and is swiftly defeated by the Central Powers

1917

February: Germany begins an unrestricted U-boat campaign

March: Collapse of the Tsarist regime in Russia

6 April: The United States declares war on Germany

16 April: The start of the Nivelle offensive

July: A final Russian offensive in Galicia fails; the Russian army begins to disintegrate

31 July to 6 November: The Third Battle of Ypres, or Battle of Passchandaele

October to December: The Caporetto Offensive, fought by German and Austrian troops against Italy

7 November: The Bolsheviks seize power in Russia

15 December: Russia and Germany agree an armistice

1918

8 January: US President Wilson announces his 14-point peace plan

3 March: The Treaty of Brest-Litovsk

21 March: The Germans launch a massive spring offensive on the Western front, driving the Allies back towards Paris

3 June: Battle of Château-Thierry

18 July: The Second Battle of the Marne

8 August: An Allied offensive begins at Amiens

19 September: Battle of Megiddo

30 September: Bulgaria signs an armistice with the Allies

28 October: Mutiny by German sailors at Kiel triggers revolutionary uprisings across Germany

30 October: The Ottoman Empire signs an armistice with the Allies

3 November: Austria-Hungary signs an armistice

9 November: Germany is declared a Republic and the Kaiser flees into exile

11 November: Germany signs an armistice; fighting stops on the Western Front

1919

28 June: The signing of the Versailles Treaty

Glossary

abdicate To step down from a throne, giving up the right to rule a country.

airship A lighter-than-air aircraft – a large balloon with an engine attached.

Allies Term used for Britain, France and the other countries fighting on their side during the war.

annex To take over territory.

armistice An agreement between two sides in a war to stop fighting so they can negotiate a peace treaty.

assassination The murder of a public figure, usually for a political motive.

atrocities Massacres or other acts of extreme brutality.

autonomy A degree of self-government falling short of full independence.

Central Powers Term used for Germany, Austria-Hungary and their allies.

coalition government A government in which several parties cooperate.

colonial empire System in which European countries such as Britain and France ruled extensive territories in other parts of the world.

Commonwealth An international association consisting of the UK together with states that were – at the time of the First War War – part of the British Empire, and dependencies.

conscription Compulsory service in the armed forces.

dominion A self-governing country in the British Empire.

ethnic divisions Conflicts or disagreements between people of different national, racial or religious groups living in the same country.

Great Depression Period of widespread economic failure from the late 1920s through the 1930s, marked by high unemployment and declining trade.

merchant ship A ship carrying cargo or passengers – not a warship.

munitions Ammunition and other equipment needed by an army.

no-man's-land The area between the front line of two armies, for example between the opposing trenches on the Western Front.

Ottoman Empire A Turkish-ruled empire that controlled much of the Middle East.

outflank To advance round the side of an enemy position.

ratify To approve something formally.

reparations Payments demanded from a defeated country by the victors to compensate for damage they have suffered in war.

revolution The overthrow of a system of government or society and its replacement by something radically different.

self-determination The principle that people should be ruled by their choice of government.

shell shock Psychological disturbance caused by prolonged exposure to bombardment.

strafing To fire on troops on the ground from an aircraft.

U-boat A German submarine.

Further Information

Books:

Holmes, Richard, *The Western Front* (BBC, 1999)

Keegan, John, *The First World War* (Hutchinson 1998)

Taylor, A. J. P., *The First World War* (Penguin, 1963)

Willmott, H. P., *First World War* (Dorling Kindersley, 2003)

Websites:

http://www.channel4.com/history

http://www.firstworldwar.com

http://www.grunts.net/wars/20thcentury/ww1

http://www.pbs.org/greatwar

http://www.spartacus.schoolnet.co.uk/FWW.htm

http://www.worldwar1.com

Index Page numbers in **bold** indicate photographs